Robert V. Conte with CJ Henderson

# Black Sabbath

### THE OZZY OSBOURNE YEARS

ROCKOGRAPHY BOOKS™ PRESENTS

# BLACK SABBATH: THE OZZY OSBOURNE YEARS

## by Robert V. Conte with CJ Henderson

Published by
STUDIO CHIKARA
244 Fifth Avenue #2464
New York, NY 10001 USA
www.stuchikara.com
www.studiochikara.net
E-mail: StuChikara@aol.com

First Edition

Robert V. Conte-Publisher
Elena Rekosh-Copy Editor
Susan Call-Proofreader
Dave Streicher-Scans
Serg Andreyev-Cover Concept
Neuwirth and Associates-Book Design
John Ostrosky-Website Director
Gary Esposito-Promotions Design
Wallace Collins III, Esq.-Business and Legal Affairs

Special thanks to Omid Yamini, John Blocher, Walter Rowan and Steve Wilson

Distributed by
Music Sales Corporation
257 Park Avenue South
New York, NY 10010 USA

Order Number: SCP 10016
ISBN 1-890313-99-8
UPC 7-52187-10016-4

Separated, Printed and Bound in the United States of America by
Phoenix Color Corp., Hagerstown, Maryland

For additional copies of BLACK SABBATH: THE OZZY OSBOURNE YEARS,
mail check or money order for $12.95 plus shipping/handling ($3.20 Domestic/$9.00 International) to the above address.

Studio Chikara wants your comments on BLACK SABBATH: THE OZZY OSBOURNE YEARS. Please E-mail them to StuChikara@aol.com

# THE MADMEN ARE BACK!

In 1969, four youths from the factory town of Birmingham, England—Ozzy Osbourne, Tony Iommi, Geezer Butler and Bill Ward—formed a group that would radically transform the world of music. Theirs was a new and unique style, a singular bombshell of furious, righteous sounds completely alien to any other popular music of its day that would eventually come to be known as "heavy metal." In 1980, Ozzy would strike out on his own, beginning an equally impressive solo career that established milestones in music history.

For thirty years, Ozzy and Black Sabbath would continue onward, twin forces riding the nightmare lightning of their own dark souls, creating the music that would inspire a thousand other bands and forever change the music industry. Many others would join them in their separate quests. Sometimes they would even reunite, creating new albums and thrilling their legions of fans with new tours, their every move cementing their indisputable role as the founding fathers of one of the greatest sounds in rock and roll history.

But how did these four men reach their unprecedented level of success? Read the true story of Black Sabbath.

# OZZY OSBOVRNE

| | |
|---|---|
| REAL NAME: | John Michael Osbourne |
| BIRTHDAY: | December 3, 1948 |
| BIRTHPLACE: | Aston, a suburb of Birmingham, England |
| INSTRUMENT: | Vocals |
| INFLUENCES: | The Beatles |
| BACKGROUND: | One of six children raised in a grim industrial town. Although both parents worked in factories, the Osbourne family was impoverished. Plagued by undiagnosed Attention Deficit Disorder (ADD) and routine physical abuse from a local gang (which included future bandmate Tony Iommi), Ozzy dropped out of high school and led a life of odd jobs and little reward. After a petty theft landed Ozzy in jail for |

# TONY IOMMI

| | |
|---|---|
| REAL NAME: | Anthony Frank Iommi |
| BIRTHDAY: | February 19, 1948 |
| BIRTHPLACE: | Aspen, The Midlands |
| INSTRUMENT: | Left-handed electric guitar |
| INFLUENCES: | Dick Richards and the Shadows, Larry Colton and Joe Pass. Tony also admired some of his contemporaries, including Brian May, Dave Gilmour and Jeff Beck. |
| BACKGROUND: | Born into a musical family that owned a sweets shop to make ends meet, Tony's original desire was to become a drummer. Tony soon retired from skinbashing in favor of an accordion and then an electric guitar. At age eighteen, Tony suffered a disabling accident at a sheet-metal |

# GEEZER BUTLER

REAL NAME: Terence Michael Butler

BIRTHDAY: July 17, 1949

BIRTHPLACE: Aston, a suburb of Birmingham, England

INSTRUMENT: Bass

INFLUENCES: Cream's Jack Bruce, Paul McCartney, Blues Breakers, Sonny Boy and Howlin' Wolf.

BACKGROUND: Geezer relied on what he called "life's defining moments"—supernatural experiences that Geezer believed shaped his destiny. When he was seven years old, a floating orb that glowed from within awakened young Terence. When Terence touched the illuminated object, it filled his head with visions of his future and a better life beyond poor, polluted Birmingham. Although the orb soon floated away, its effects upon Terence would last for decades to come.

# BILL WARD

REAL NAME: William Thomas Ward

BIRTHDAY: May 5, 1948

BIRTHPLACE: Aston, a suburb of Birmingham, England

INSTRUMENT: Drums

INFLUENCES: Gene Krupa, Led Zeppelin's John Bonham and The Who's Keith Moon.

BACKGROUND: Like his fellow bandmates, Bill Ward spent much of his teens drifting from job to job, searching for his ultimate calling. Eventually Bill became an assistant truck driver, until his employer chastised him once too often for hitting the dashboard with his drumsticks. Fed up with being treated as an inferior, Bill announced his resignation by jumping out of the vehicle while it was driving on a major road. After that, Bill decided that rock and roll was his ticket out of Birmingham and vowed never to work for anyone ever again.

As youngsters, Ozzy Osbourne and Tony Iommi first meet at Birchfield School in England. Then sixteen-year-old Tony and his gang overheard young Ozzy singing The Beatles' "I Want to Hold Your Hand" to himself during recess. Tony assaulted him while his gang circled around their victim yelling, "Oz-brain! Oz-brain!" Suffering a severe beating, Ozzy swore he would join the Royal Air Force so he wouldn't have to deal with Tony ever again. Ozzy did not join the RAF, however, so it was destined that his path would cross with Tony's once more. . .

Three years later, eighteen-year-old Geezer Butler was searching for a vocalist. Reading posts at a local music store, Geezer spotted an advertisement that interested him: "Ozzy Zig, vocalist, requires band. Owns own P.A." Since public address systems were hard to come by, Geezer determined that Ozzy was his man. Ozzy showed up at Geezer's place with a buzzcut, reeking of the slaughterhouse where he worked. The smell of blood and animal fear must have been intoxicating, for within seconds, Ozzy and Geezer were bandmates in a group named Rare Breed.

Meanwhile, Tony Iommi joined a blues band named The Rest that would soon recruit drummer Bill Ward. With singer Chris Smith, The Rest toured throughout Carlisle, Northern England.

Soon The Rest was transformed into Mythology and, although they developed a solid reputation wherever they played, the band could barely afford to eat. Tony and Bill knew that Mythology was not destined to last very long the way it was going, so they decided to start fresh and return to Birmingham.

Tony Iommi and Bill Ward, starving and desperate to form a new band, returned to their hometown hoping to find a bassist and vocalist. Scanning the local newspapers, they stumbled across a familiar ad: "Ozzy Zig, vocalist, requires band. Owns own P.A." Reluctantly, Tony took Bill to Ozzy's house—concerned that this Ozzy was the same one he bullied in high school. Tony's fear was soon realized, but he and Ozzy quickly worked out their differences in hopes of forming a band that would take over the world.

Thus were the seeds planted for one of the greatest bands of all time: Tony, Ozzy, Geezer and Bill—along with a slide guitarist and a sax player—rehearsed and developed a unique sound blending blues and jazz. Within days, the Polka Tulk Blues Band (Ozzy took the name from a local Indian clothing emporium) toured in Carlisle with over a dozen songs to capitalize on Mythology's following. Although the band's name and their additional musicians did not last long, Tony, Geezer, Ozzy and Bill were on their way to making rock and roll history.

Soon the awkwardly named Polka Tulk Blues Band was renamed Earth. The band's jazz-blues style was discontinued in favor of a new harder-than-blues, louder-than-pop sound. Ozzy, Geezer, Tony and Bill's new "gloom and doom" music soon became their much-talked-about trademark. Earth's rising popularity was noticed by a promoter, who decided to approach them with an offer. In exchange for a night's worth of food and drink, Earth would perform as the supporting act for Ten Years After. Eager for the exposure that would come from opening for a popular recording group, Earth happily agreed.

Audience reaction to Earth was superb. After Earth opened for Jethro Tull in December 1968, Tull vocalist Ian Anderson offered Tony the opportunity to join the band. Tony agreed, simultaneously destroying Earth and the hopes of its remaining members as he abandoned them all. But during filming of the Rolling Stones' *Rock 'N' Roll Circus*, Iommi felt mistreated and abruptly left Jethro Tull. Tony went back to Ozzy, Bill and Geezer, vowing he would never leave the band again. With renewed determination, Earth set out to become as popular as The Beatles.

By 1969, Earth had earned a solid reputation throughout England as one of the most original-sounding local bands around. But their popularity suffered a setback when the band's self-proclaimed "manager" booked them a disastrous show in their hometown of Birmingham. While performing, Ozzy noticed that the audience was less than receptive to the band's music. Moments later,

it was discovered that another band named Earth was to play the same bill that night. Embarrassed, the group dropped the name Earth (and its manager).

While rehearsing new material, the band formerly named Earth experienced a supernatural occurrence. Geezer and Tony were playing new riffs for Ozzy and Bill when, much to everyone's surprise, they both strummed the same notes at the same tempo—although neither had ever before heard the other one play the piece! Convinced that this was an omen, Geezer christened the song and the group Black Sabbath, based on the title of a 1935 Boris Karloff movie (Geezer's favorite horror film). Soon, Black Sabbath's musicianship rose to new heights as the band grew tighter, louder and more determined than ever.

Black Sabbath's name and sound spread all over the local music scene. Soon they were approached by promoter/manager Jim Simpson, who booked them at various European shows, including The Star Club in Germany (where Sabbath was pleased to break The Beatles' record for longest-held house attendance). Although Sabbath played up to seven sets a day, they were still barely able to feed themselves. Disillusioned and broke, Sabbath quickly accepted the chance to record a cover of Crow's "Evil Woman (Don't Play Your Games with Me)." The single gained little attention but did help earn Sabbath a recording contract with Vertigo Records.

With high enthusiasm and a mind-staggering, minuscule budget of £600.00 (about $900.00 U.S. dollars), Black Sabbath recorded

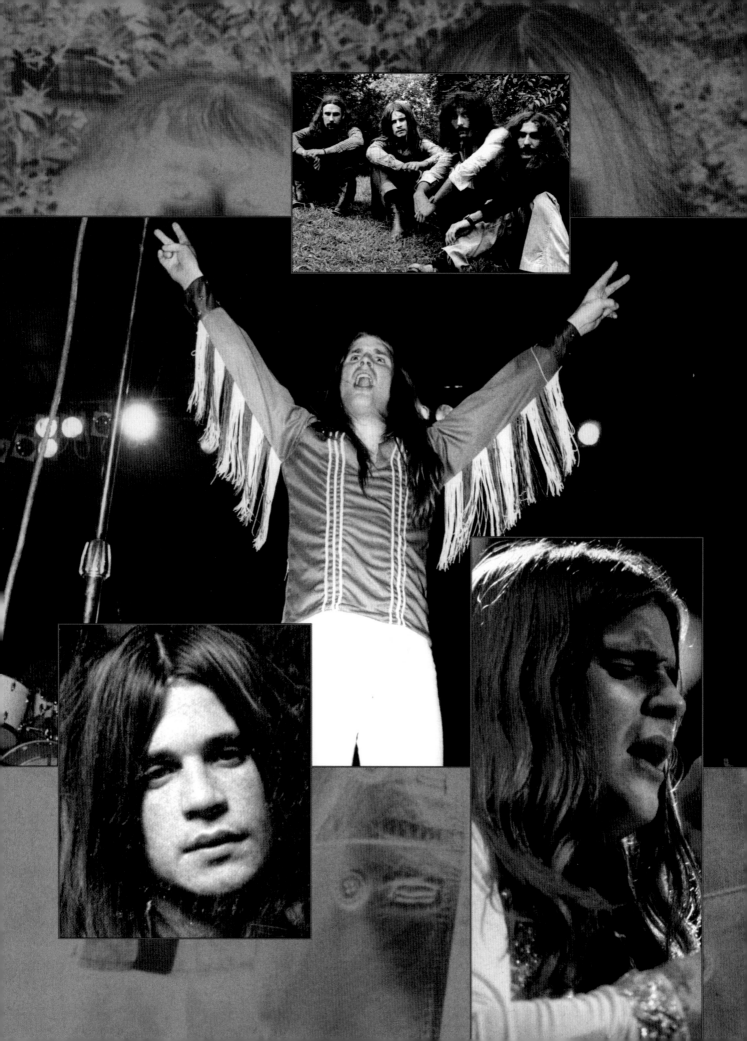

their first album in an unbelievable twelve hours spread over only three days (on an eight-track machine, no less) at Regent Sound in London. On Friday the thirteenth, February 1970, the group's premier album, *Black Sabbath,* was released in the U.K. Controversy erupted surrounding the album's gatefold artwork—an upside down cross—which prevented critics from reviewing the album objectively.

Indeed, the reviews were depressingly savage, but Sabbath's audiences were entranced by the band's eerie combination of "live" drums, guitar, bass, harmonica and vocals. The album might have garnered the critics' hatred, but critics rarely buy records. Despite the media's dire warnings, the album sold steadily, easily reaching number eight on the British charts, where it stayed for six months.

As Sabbath toured Europe supporting their first album, the band was approached by a Satanic cult that asked them to perform on their "Walpurgis Nacht," or "Night of Satan," to be held at Stonehenge. Sabbath declined the invitation and was subsequently threatened with a hex. Alec Sanders, then the head witch of the British Isles, informed the band that the only way to nullify the curse would be to wear crosses around their necks. For years, the band wore silver crosses made for them by Ozzy's father. This new look—along with the band's completely unique music—helped solidify Black Sabbath's image.

Based on the group's experiences with the occult and the subsequent cancellation of their first U.S. tour due to Charles Manson's recent satanic murdering spree, Black Sabbath debuted "Walpurgis" to hundreds of unsuspecting soldiers at an American Air Base in mid-1970. The crowd roared its approval over the track. Inspired anew by Vietnam and the overall tragedy of war, Geezer rewrote the song's lyrics and retitled the now-famous track "War Pigs." Upon finishing this mini-tour, Ozzy, Geezer, Bill and Tony were ready and eager to record another album.

Black Sabbath had a wealth of new, original material when they entered Regent Sound and Island Studios in July 1970 to record their next album. Again they worked at lightning speed. Recorded in only four days, the band's second disc—originally entitled *War Pigs*—had even more of a wicked, heavier sound than its predecessor. Warner Brothers Records (Sabbath's new U.S. label) decided the title was far too risqué (and too reminiscent of the Vietnam War) for the American public and quickly sought to rename the album. Before its release in September 1970, *War Pigs* was retitled *Paranoid*. With no time to change the cover art, the sword-wielding sci-fi barbarian designed to go with the title "War Pigs," ended up doing double duty.

"Paranoid"—titled after a "throwaway" song written in only four minutes—reached number one on the U.K. charts in October 1970. Sabbath's second release would prove to become one of the most influential albums in rock and roll history, spawning several classics such as "Iron Man," "Fairies Wear Boots," "Electric Funeral" and the title track, which reached number four on the U.K. singles charts. Ozzy, Tony, Geezer and Bill made their first British television

appearance on "Top of the Pops" before thousands of soon-to-be Sabbath fans.

As Black Sabbath's success grew and their popularity increased worldwide, it became apparent that manager Jim Simpson wasn't sharing the wealth—not with the band, anyway. When Ozzy, Tony, Bill and Geezer inquired about their finances, Simpson assured them that everything was fine. Sadly, it would be years before Sabbath discovered the truth: Simpson had secretly decided to keep his clients' fortune for himself.

Black Sabbath finally had an opportunity to tour the U.S. where they supported Canned Heat on Halloween, 1970. During the show, electrical wiring brought from England but not properly prepared for American voltage levels caused some of the band's equipment to explode on stage. While Sabbath stood shell shocked, the audience cheered excitedly, believing the sparks and explosions all to be part of the act! Although pyrotechnics would be used on future tours, Sabbath's main priority was always to concentrate on their live performances. Later, Sabbath opened for Rod Stewart and the Faces, Mountain and Grand Funk Railroad where their popularity rose above the headlining acts.

After completing exhausting tours across both sides of the Atlantic Ocean, Black Sabbath had amassed many road-related experiences. Inspired to create new material, Ozzy, Geezer, Bill and Tony recorded *Master of Reality* at various studios throughout England with one purpose: to create the heaviest-sounding rock and roll album ever made! The result was just that. Featuring "Sweet Leaf" and "Lord of this World," *Master of Reality* was released in July 1971 and reached number five on the British charts and number eight in the U.S. The album also gave the world "Children of the Grave," one of the band's best-known numbers and one of the many classics to be performed by almost every one of Sabbath's future incarnations.

Returning to the U.S. as headliners, Black Sabbath suffered some bizarre, unexpected effects of their dark unworldly image. Before a concert in Memphis, Tennessee, the band's dressing rooms were covered in crosses drawn with animal blood. During the same performance, a Satanist attempted to kill Tony with a knife on stage, claiming he would sacrifice the guitarist's soul to the Devil. After the show, a coven of witches waited outside Sabbath's hotel in hopes of being "saved" by the group. Fearful of being mobbed, Geezer chanted a fake hex to clear away the crowd.

By 1972, the members of Black Sabbath were living examples of the ultimate hard-rock lifestyle—sex, drugs and rock and roll, and the more, the better. These attributes influenced the writing and recording of the band's fourth album, originally entitled *Snowblind*. Drug references throughout this latest offering concerned Sabbath's uptight record label. The proposed cocaine-referenced title was quickly changed to *Black Sabbath Vol. 4*. Despite its mundane name, Sabbath's newest album became another instant Platinum smash.

The strain of constant touring began to negatively affect the members of Black Sabbath, however. Psychological pressures and physical ailments forced the cancellation and rescheduling of several concert dates. After a much-needed rest, Black Sabbath resumed touring in 1973. Some shows on the group's British tour were recorded for a much-demanded live album. Although fan interest was high, the idea was ultimately scrapped. (Some of these recordings were finally featured on 1980's *Live At Last*, however.) During this

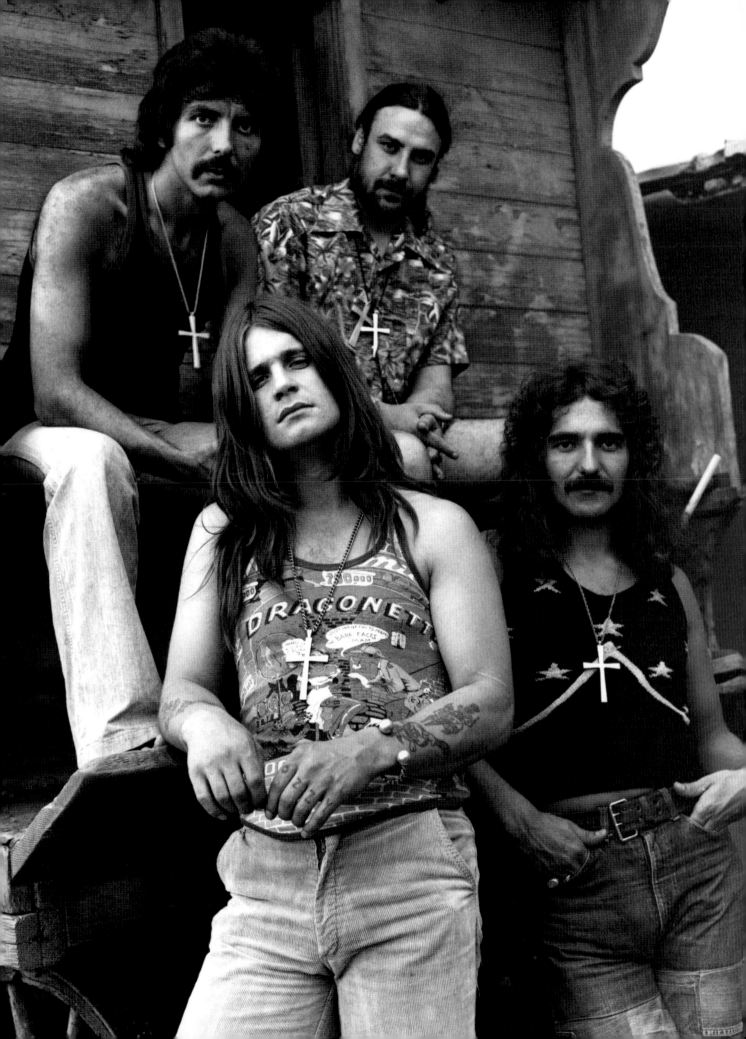

period, Black Sabbath changed management from Jim Simpson to Patrick Meehan, whose involvement with the group was short-lived.

Geezer's encounters with the supernatural continued. During recording of *Sabbath Bloody Sabbath* in Bel Air, the bassist felt an ominous presence fill his bedroom. He looked up to see several specters glaring at him from above with overpowering effect. Awash with fear, he immediately awakened Bill, Tony and Ozzy to tell them what had happened. Geezer soon discovered that all of his fellow bandmates had experienced similar events. This period in Sabbath's career served as inspiration for the *Sabbath Bloody Sabbath* album's cover artwork, created by famed film poster painter Drew Struzan.

Exhausted from the rigors of touring, Black Sabbath returned to England in 1973 to complete *Sabbath Bloody Sabbath*. This period marked the longest period in the band's career when they did not take to the stage. But just because Sabbath had decided to take a break didn't mean that the types of strange occurrences they had discussed in America were over.

Inside the castle where the band lived and recorded, Ozzy fell into a deep sleep by a lit fireplace. His blankets caught fire and, if not for Tony and Geezer smelling smoke, Ozzy would have been burned to death. To Sabbath, it was obvious that a dark, ominous cloud was looming over them. Although *Sabbath Bloody Sabbath* was the most critically acclaimed album of their entire career, the band unanimously decided it was time to end their dabbling in the occult once and for all. Merely cutting their ties with Satan could not banish the greatest disaster ahead of them, however.

By 1974, Black Sabbath started to crumble from within. Ozzy was dissatisfied with the group's musical experimentation, which was causing Sabbath to drift farther and farther away from their signature hard-and-heavy sound. Also, at the same time, Ozzy began a downward spiral into drugs and alcohol that would continue throughout his remaining tenure with the group (and for years after). Sabbath soon changed managers—once again—to Don Arden. Although times looked gloomy for Sabbath's internal structure, the group headlined 1974's infamous California Jam in front of over 400,000 fans who showered them with adoration.

While touring in the U.S., Ozzy was handed a subpoena from Black Sabbath's former manager, Jim Simpson, who accused the group of wrongful termination. It was soon discovered that Simpson had not paid Sabbath millions of dollars in royalties they had earned since the release of their 1970 self-titled debut. Thus began a two-year-long legal battle that temporarily forced Tony, Bill, Geezer and Ozzy to stop touring. And Ozzy's previous descent into the world of binge alcohol and drugs led to his further isolation from the group.

Unable to tour due to the seemingly endless legal dispute between their former and current managers, Black Sabbath decided there was no reason their time should go

completely to waste. If they couldn't tour, they would record their next album, *Sabotage* (created at England's Morgan Studios). During this period the group grew bitter toward the music business—a mood evident in the album's title and most of its songs. Even though it took over a year to complete, however, *Sabotage* included some of Sabbath's best music ever, including "Symptom of the Universe," "Hole in the Sky" and "Supertzar."

Despite the circumstances that gave it birth, *Sabotage* was considered to be Sabbath's peak album by fans, critics and the group themselves. Although many felt that *Sabbath Bloody Sabbath* marked the beginning of the band losing its way, *Sabotage* proved that Black Sabbath was still the heaviest of the heavy, the metal masters who created rock and roll's most unique sound.

With *Sabotage* reaching number seven in the U.K. and number twenty-eight in the U.S., Black Sabbath's legal problems were soon behind them. (Sadly, the band was forced to pay former manager Jim

Simpson a large percentage of what little royalties remained from their early days.) Sabbath's 1975 tour became the pinnacle of the group's live career. It was an unprecedented period, one marked not only by Sabbath's own success, but also by the abandonment of the playing field by much of their competition.

Groups like Deep Purple and Led Zeppelin began changing their sounds radically. To all intents and purposes, Sabbath should have been the happiest band around. However, the group's internal personality conflicts reached an all-time high at this point, poisoning what should have been the high point of their careers. Ozzy and Tony fought regularly about Sabbath's musical direction, Ozzy's continually worsening drug abuse and who should take center stage during their performances. (Unbelievably, the talented but somewhat stiff Tony demanded the center stage spot when they performed live, relegating the wildly animated Ozzy to one side.)

I n 1976, Black Sabbath relocated to the United States (to escape Britain's confiscatory tax laws) to record their seventh album, *Technical Ecstasy*. Unlike the group's previous efforts, this record was distinctly un-Sabbath and led to the group's first decline in popularity. Although *Technical Ecstasy* featured heavy tracks like "Dirty Women," "Back Street Kids" and "Rock and Roll Doctor," its overall sound was bitterly

disappointing to Sabbath's hard-core fans. This, of course, was exactly what Ozzy had feared and why he had battled so long and hard with Tony over tampering unduly with the group's singular sound. Extremely unhappy with the album—and the group—Ozzy abruptly quit Black Sabbath in late 1977.

The remaining members of Sabbath were now faced with the unthinkable. Ozzy Osbourne—the group's frontman and most popular member—had resigned. With work to do and commitments to him, Tony, Geezer and Bill couldn't waste any time finding a replacement. Vocalist Dave Walker, who had once fronted Savoy Brown and Fleetwood Mac, was hired to replace Ozzy. After a single unsuccessful appearance on BBC television, it became clear that Sabbath's newest member did not have any of the much-needed stage charisma that Ozzy exploited so easily.

Black Sabbath was in trouble. The band desperately needed Ozzy back if it was to survive. In early 1978, Sabbath persuaded Ozzy to rejoin the group for their highly anticipated "Tenth Anniversary Tour." Tony, Bill and Geezer had songs prepared for a new album that was to be recorded with Dave Walker on vocals. Ozzy bluntly refused to sing material meant for another vocalist, so the tracks were scrapped and the band hastily recorded *Never Say Die* at Sounds Interchange Studio in Toronto, Canada.

*Never Say Die* was released in October 1978, reaching number twelve in the U.K. and number sixty-nine in the U.S. Unfortunately, the album was the original group's most unfocused, least successful effort to date. The magic that once was Black Sabbath looked to be ebbing away. It was all too clear to Tony, Geezer and Bill that they had to make an immediate decision regarding the band's future—and Ozzy's ultimate fate.

Although Ozzy had returned to Black Sabbath, his relationship with his bandmates had been severely damaged. During the group's "Tenth Anniversary Tour" it became obvious to them all that Ozzy's heart simply was not with Sabbath anymore. Ozzy didn't show up at a Nashville, Tennessee concert, forcing its cancellation (he fell asleep in the wrong hotel room and couldn't be found, causing speculation by the authorities that he had been kidnapped). This latest outrage showed the rest of the group what they had to do to ensure Sabbath's survival.

Tony, Geezer and Bill called Ozzy to a final meeting in early 1979. Bill was selected to give Ozzy the bad news: effective immediately, Ozzy Osbourne was no longer a member of Black Sabbath. Devastated (but not entirely surprised), Ozzy swore that he would rule the world without them. Out of loyalty to Geezer from their early days as members of Rare Breed, Ozzy invited him to form a new group. Geezer refused. With that, Ozzy left his former bandmates to themselves. After twelve years, after selling more than eight-million albums together and thrilling the world with the most innovative music of all time, the original Black Sabbath was suddenly no more. . .

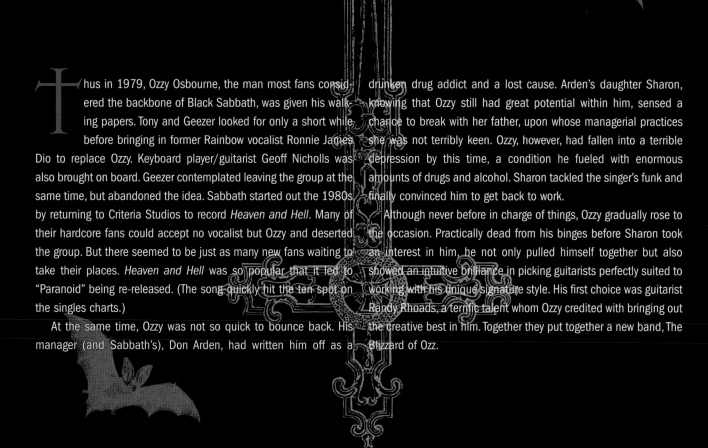

Thus in 1979, Ozzy Osbourne, the man most fans considered the backbone of Black Sabbath, was given his walking papers. Tony and Geezer looked for only a short while before bringing in former Rainbow vocalist Ronnie James Dio to replace Ozzy. Keyboard player/guitarist Geoff Nicholls was also brought on board. Geezer contemplated leaving the group at the same time, but abandoned the idea. Sabbath started out the 1980s by returning to Criteria Studios to record *Heaven and Hell*. Many of their hardcore fans could accept no vocalist but Ozzy and deserted the group. But there seemed to be just as many new fans waiting to take their places. *Heaven and Hell* was so popular that it led to "Paranoid" being re-released. (The song quickly hit the ten spot on the singles charts.)

At the same time, Ozzy was not so quick to bounce back. His manager (and Sabbath's), Don Arden, had written him off as a drunken drug addict and a lost cause. Arden's daughter Sharon, knowing that Ozzy still had great potential within him, sensed a chance to break with her father, upon whose managerial practices she was not terribly keen. Ozzy, however, had fallen into a terrible depression by this time, a condition he fueled with enormous amounts of drugs and alcohol. Sharon tackled the singer's funk and finally convinced him to get back to work.

Although never before in charge of things, Ozzy gradually rose to the occasion. Practically dead from his binges before Sharon took an interest in him, he not only pulled himself together but also showed an intuitive brilliance in picking guitarists perfectly suited to working with his unique signature style. His first choice was guitarist Randy Rhoads, a terrific talent whom Ozzy credited with bringing out the creative best in him. Together they put together a new band, The Blizzard of Ozz.

At first, no record companies would talk with Sharon and Ozzy. They went from label to label, desperate to put together a recording deal. Finally, the new Jet Records offered to release Ozzy's album for a measly sixty-five thousand dollars! The album, of course, was a resounding smash hit upon its release, jamming the Top Ten in the British Isles and the number twenty-one spot in America. It went Quadruple Platinum in an incredibly short amount of time.

Jet Records and its distributor, CBS/Columbia, were now congratulating themselves for bringing Ozzy aboard. During a meeting of Ozzy, Sharon and over twenty company executives, a flock of doves was released to make an impression. During the stunt, Ozzy decided to "make an impression" himself—he bit the head off one of the doves and dropped its bloody, still-flapping body on the meeting table. As horrified executives threw up, Ozzy was banned from the CBS/Columbia building. None of this stopped the delicate executives from raking in the cash with both hands as the star's second album, *Diary of A Madman*, also went Quadruple Platinum.

Events did not unfold quite as smoothly for the Ozz's old mates, however. Things became confused as the band shrank and grew repeatedly after Ozzy was fired. Nicholls and Dio stifled the first of several talent hemorrhages, but soon another of the group's original members was driven from the fold. Bill Ward, finding he could no longer control his drinking binges, took a leave of absence to enter detox. To fill the void, Sabbath brought in ex-Derringer drummer Vinnie Appice.

*Live At Last* came out during this period, much to the band's consternation. Seven years previously, Sabbath had been planning to create a live album. Their manager at that time was the eventually dismissed Patrick Meehan. The album, although a remarkably solid representation of the group's live sound, was released without Sabbath's permission by their U.K. record label.

More internal problems among the remaining band members surfaced in 1982. During the *Mob Rules* tour, Tony felt that the group's new frontman, Ronnie James Dio, was unjustly using the event to promote his upcoming solo album. Not long after that, Sabbath announced that a new singer would be taking Dio's place—ex–Deep Purple vocalist Ian Gillan. Vinnie Appice left with Dio, which was actually fortuitous since it made way for a partially recovered Bill Ward to return. Ward felt up to doing studio work only, however, so in the end he was replaced by ELO's Bev Bevan so that Sabbath could tour once more.

Black Sabbath then released the album *Born Again,* which hit the number four spot on the charts, the first time Sabbath had made it that close to the top in a decade. There were many disputes over whether a Black Sabbath without Ozzy Osbourne was really Sabbath, but there was no denying that the band still had the power to draw crowds and sell records.

Things did not stabilize, however, and the band's musical chairs continued. First, in 1984, Ian Gillan left to rejoin a reuniting Deep Purple. Dave Donato took his place for a brief stint on vocals. Jeff Fenholt, whose stint was even shorter, replaced Donato. This merry-go-round of changing band members contin-

ued throughout the production of the group's next seven albums. The lock-iron continuity and singular body punch of the original Black Sabbath was lost as their sound slowly crumbled bit by bit. During this time, the band became erratic, and worse, lazy. Albums were put together without care or feeling. Unbelievably, the legendary Black Sabbath was on autopilot and was spiraling down toward the ground at a terrible speed. Although their core audience was still vast and fiercely loyal, the numbers did begin to measurably trickle away.

During the same period, tragedy descended upon Ozzy once more. In 1982, after making only two albums together, the Ozz was separated in the most terrible of ways from the man who helped him reinvent himself so completely. Randy Rhoads and several friends were flying over Ozzy's property in a small private aircraft. They flew over his tour bus three times without cause to be concerned. But on a fourth pass disaster struck. In an instant, without warning, the plane crashed and the talented Randy Rhoads was killed. His sound and his friendship were both of vast importance to Ozzy. For the time being, the survivors of the tragedy were torn asunder. Ozzy was so completely crushed by the depressing event that he considered leaving the business completely.

Only a few months later, though, the Ozz married his manager and companion, Sharon Arden. Unbelievably, despite his days with Black Sabbath and his enormous success with The Blizzard of Ozz, the singer was nearly broke. Don Arden's leeching contract had taken practically everything. Having learned a great deal at her father's side, however, Sharon managed to wrest control of Ozzy's career away from Daddy Dearest.

Part of the deal that was struck called for Ozzy to enter rehab. Wanting to make a go of his new marriage (and somewhat tired of the never-ending, debilitating flow of alcohol and cocaine), Ozzy agreed without putting up much of a fight. In 1984, he checked himself into the Betty Ford Clinic with the intention of finally cleaning up his act before he destroyed himself and his future.

After his stay, Ozzy was soon clean and clear and back to work. His solo career skyrocketed, while Black Sabbath, although still producing albums on a regular basis, accomplished nothing extraordinary. Sadly, there were no signs of change on the horizon. Then, in 1985, the world of rock and roll was given a gift beyond measure.

Visionary promoter Bob Geldorf put together the legendary Live Aid concert. He tried to bring together every major band the world had ever known in their original incarnations. In the case of

Ozzy's heroes, The Beatles, he proposed that the late John Lennon's son Julian sit in for his father. The Beatles turned down Geldorf. So did others. Many did not, however, and Sabbath was one of them.

Finally, on July 13, 1985, in Philadelphia, Pennsylvania, the magic began. The city of brotherly love was blessed with the reunion not only of The Who but also of Crosby, Stills, Nash & Young, those members of Led Zeppelin still breathing, and, of course, Black Sabbath. Ozzy Osbourne, Geezer Butler, Tony Iommi and a freshly sober Bill Ward took the stage together once more. It was a night whose worth was beyond measure to those in attendance. Sabbath rocked as if they had never stopped playing together. Hope ran rampant throughout fandom that this epic gift was but a signpost toward a future in which the gods of heavy metal would finally reunite.

But instead, the concert was merely a testament to the group's professionalism as performers. Although their resounding success was a surprise even to them, after the show everyone went their separate ways once more. And worse yet for Sabbath's fans, even Geezer left the group at this point. The band played on with only Iommi left from the original days. He was backed up Dave Spitz (bass), Geoff Nicholls (keyboard), Eric Singer (drums) and Glenn Hughes (vocals).

The new group produced an album released under the embarrassingly awkward title Black Sabbath Featuring Tony Iommi: Seventh Star. The world's greatest heavy metal band, the group that started it all, was reduced to a franchise. The band's tour was a dismal whisper of the past. Fans who could remember Ozzy's performances were now saddled with watching an overweight, out-of-tune Hughes. Ray Gillen replaced the pathetic frontman after only a few tour dates. Gillen lasted through the tour and began work with the others on Sabbath's next album, but he had to be replaced halfway through the recording, his vocals stripped out and replaced by those of Tony Martin.

It was not Sabbath's finest hour. But they weren't the only ones having problems. At this point both Sabbath and Ozzy were experiencing difficulty in creating separate identities. The numbers made famous in the band's early days—especially those from the first three albums—had become "Ozzy's songs." The tunes simply could not be sung by anyone else in the known universe. The Ozz was the owner of the most unusual voice in rock and roll history. Although he admittedly sang in a virtual monotone, he did so with such a curling, edged sound that it stirred his audiences beyond reason. No one else was capable of making his material their own.

On the other hand, Ozzy's new band couldn't play a set without crushing demands for the inclusion of Black Sabbath songs. As well received as they and their new material were by the public, the audience wanted to hear Ozzy singing "War Pigs" and "Sweet Leaf," and justifiably so. Still, this was merely a mild ego blow for the Ozz, whereas Black Sabbath found itself almost falling apart. The group's 1989 American tour was a fairly unsuccessful experience.

Still, thanks to the magic of the Live Aid concert, some of the old hatchets were finally buried with professionalism and civility. The old animosities were finally over.

Almost.

Shortly after Ronnie James Dio returned to Sabbath to record *Dehumanizer* in 1992, they are asked to open for Ozzy's band during their "No More Tours" tour. Dio found this offer offensive and quit Sabbath. Rob Halford (formerly of Judas Priest) replaced him, and the shows were a rousing success. This was the closest Sabbath audiences had gotten to their dream in years. But for these loyal fans, the best was yet to come.

In Costa Mesa, California, during the last show of the tour, Ozzy thrilled the crowds by joining Black Sabbath on stage for four numbers—"Fairies Wear Boots," "Paranoid," "Black Sabbath" and "Iron Man." Electricity filled the air. It was the first taste of the true Masters of Reality for the fans in years, and the crowd showed its appreciation by blowing the roof off with thunderous cheers and applause.

Suddenly, all of fandom was again talking reunion. This was it—nothing could stop it. It had to be, man. And why not? Ozzy was on top of the world. In 1993, he took a Grammy for the Best Metal Performance award for the year—"I Don't Want to Change the World" from the *Live and Loud* album. There was plenty of fuel, and the fans kept stoking the fires for the reunion they were desperate to experience.

Sadly, however, the sky once more crashed in on the world of metal. First, the Ozz decided not only that the idea of returning to Black Sabbath did not suit him, but also that performing in general left him cold. In a move that stunned his worldwide audience, he actually retired from the stage completely.

Then, to make matters worse, at the end of the tour Geezer again departed from Sabbath, leaving Iommi as the lone Master. Ozzy was gone from music, and Butler and Ward were gone from Sabbath. Finally, most people accepted the dark inevitability they had dreaded for so long. . .

There would be no reunion—there would never again be a Black Sabbath worth knowing.

This time, it was over, and Sabbath's fans were finally willing to admit it. To the world at large, it seemed that all that was left was to grab up the woeful hammer and chisel and start carving the band's headstone.

But nothing lasts forever, including despair. In 1996, Ozzy snarled and awakened, hungry for the spotlight once again. He created Ozzfest—the most successful tour extravaganza of its time! Returning to the stage, he played once more with Geezer Butler, and the world of metal rose from near death. The event was such a major turning point in music, and the demand for a new tour was so overwhelming, that even Ozzy finally bent to the will of the people.

In 1997, the new Ozzfest topped the last. The second tour was the high point of rock and roll for that summer. Nothing else came close to touching it, including the corporate shill machine, Lollapallooza. The only thing that could make the dark magic in the air more complete was the return of the original Black Sabbath. Fate cannot be denied, and plans were made to bring Sabbath back together at last.

December 4 and 5, 1997—Birmingham, England. In the place it all started, it all came back together. Weeks of sequestered rehearsal were put in to make everything perfect. And then, finally at long last, after not just years, but decades of anticipation, the great moment comes: the original Black Sabbath is reunited! There are some fans so old they are already in their graves. Others so young they didn't even exist the last time Sabbath toured the world. For them this is the moment decreed by the Fates who weave the tapestry of human destiny.

At the appointed time, in the dank and gloomy factory town that started it all, it happens. Hell's four horsemen mount their steeds once more. The crowd cheers. The skies darken. Metal lives! The one and only Black Sabbath is together on stage once more. The Devil dances and the nights blaze with ebony flame!

The next year saw Ozzfest '98 come to America. More than fifteen bands filled the ticket. Ozzy and his brood took the main stage, headlining the metalfest with bands like Coal Chamber, Limp Bizkit and Megadeth. Motorhead was the main draw on the second stage, supported by the Melvins, Monster Voodoo Machine, Ultraspank and others. Black Sabbath didn't play at Ozzfest. Instead, Ozzy took the stage all alone. With Ozzy performing solo again, would all hopes for another Black Sabbath reunion be for naught?

In October 1998, *Reunion* was released. This live album (generated from Sabbath's reunion shows in Birmingham, England) included two all-new studio cuts by the original group—the first time Ozzy, Geezer, Tony and Bill had recorded together in twenty years. Shortly thereafter, Black Sabbath announced their "Reunion" tour. From November 1998 through February 1999, the entire country was blanketed with ultra-successful, sold-out shows featuring Britain's Masters of Metal. After a brief rest,

Sabbath hit the road again for their "Last Supper" tour—the highlight of Ozzfest '99.

Another highlight occurred at the 1999 Grammy Awards, where Black Sabbath's live version of "Iron Man" (featured on *Reunion*) was nominated by the National Academy of Recording Arts and Sciences for Best Metal Performance—and won. It would be the band's first-ever Grammy.

Then, in December 1999, Black Sabbath returned to Europe for one last time—purposely selecting smaller venues so die-hard fans would see the greatest show ever. True to their word, Ozzy, Geezer, Tony and Bill performed perhaps the best shows of their careers—shows fans will still remember when they're moldering in their graves.

Sadly, all good things must come to an end. Picking the winter solstice, the calendar date when the days are the shortest and the nights extend longer than any other time of the year—the fateful moment when darkness rules on Earth—Black Sabbath returned to Birmingham, England for two final performances.

It is a blockbuster event. The group commanded the cosmos on both dates. The old magic was there for every note. Ozzy, Tony, Geezer and Bill had done it. For the boy who ran the ad "Ozzy Zig, vocalist, requires band. Owns own P.A." and the others who joined him, the circle was now complete. They created a new sound out of the pain and bleak despair of Birmingham, giving the world something it had never seen before, but which it recognized immediately from the burning truth that raged within it. Like Pablo Picasso, like Robert E. Howard, they gave birth to an art form that did not exist before their coming. As its master, they have no equal.

We have been told that December 21 and 22, 1999, marked the last time the original Black Sabbath will ever play together.

Of course, we've been told that before. . .

# SELECTED BLACK SABBATH DISCOGRAPHY

All official Black Sabbath releases, as available today on compact disc, featuring Ozzy Osbourne on vocals.

| Album | Released |
| --- | --- |
| BLACK SABBATH | Feb. 1970 |
| PARANOID | Sept. 1970 |
| MASTER OF REALITY | Aug. 1971 |
| BLACK SABBATH Vol. 4 | Sept. 1972 |
| SABBATH BLOODY SABBATH | Oct. 1973 |
| SABOTAGE | Sept. 1975 |
| WE SOLD OUR SOUL FOR ROCK AND ROLL | Dec. 1975 |
| TECHNICAL ECSTASY | Oct. 1976 |
| NEVER SAY DIE | Oct. 1978 |
| LIVE AT LAST | June 1980 |
| REUNION | Oct. 1998 |

# BLACK SABBATH

## 1969-1999